Meditation

Through Natural Pure Awareness Meditation, You May Look Into Your Own Mind, Relax Into Pure Being, And Learn More About Who You Really Are

(Hypnosis And Guided Imagery For The Relief Of Stress, The Promotion Of Confidence, And The Achievement Of Inner Peace)

HannesSchmid

TABLE OF CONTENT

Introduction 1

Restoring Health To The Throat Chakra 12

The Power That Comes From Being Spiritual. 20

Light Therapy For The Healing Of The Chakras
.... 30

Through The Use Of Color Therapy, Your Chakras Will Be Strengthened And Rebalanced.
.... 35

What Exactly Are The Chakras? 51

Practices For Opening And Balancing The Heart Chakra 59

Relationship Between Two People Based On Their Chakras 63

The "Anahata" Chakra Is Located In The Center Of The Heart 69

A Glance At The Contemporary World 78

How To Awaken Your Dormant Root Chakras 82

Your Own Internal Energy Structure 89

The Most Efficient Techniques To Rid Yourself Of The Sins And Bad Energies That Have Accumulated Through Time 98

The Chakra Located In The Navel Region......103

Crown Chakra Basics 109

The Value Of Restoring Balance To Your Chakras 113

Manifestations Of An Unbalanced Sacral Chakra And Its Symptoms 119

Symptoms Of A Disrupted Energy Balance In The Heart Chakra 124

Understanding Chakras 127

The Seven Chakras And The Functions Relating To Each Of Them...132

This Is The Throat Chakra. 147

Having Firsthand Experience With The Strength Of Love 150

Activating And Deactivating Your Chakras ...155

Introduction

Science tells us that the fight or flight sensations we experience when we encounter potential threats (fight encourages us to approach the potentially benign situation and flight prompts us run away), come from the almond-shaped part of the brain called the amygdala. Science also suggests that our amygdala's impulsivity, which occurs when our amygdala sends messages without first consulting the logical part of our brain, is why we inappropriately choose to fight when we should actually take flight. Those who are believers in chakras, on the other hand, provide a quite different explanation for this phenomena. Instead, they explain that the sense of "fight or flight" that we experience when we come across possible dangers comes from a specific energy source inside our bodies called the Base; it is the Base that regulates our impulses to survive, not the amygdala. Therefore, it is due of the imbalance in our Base, which is creating unjustified fits of hostility or fury, that we make irrational decisions to fight instead of flee in unsuitable situations.

Intriguingly, each of these perspectives on the human body have a fundamental aspect in common: the want to demystify and explain the natural processes that take place inside the human body in accordance with one's particular set of beliefs. This is a shared goal shared by scientists and spiritual people alike. The main difference is that spiritual people equate fight or flight with the energy node in our body known as the Base, while scientists correlate fight or flight with a sequence of responses that occur in our brain.

There is no reason for concern on the part of those who are not aware with the notion of chakras. The fundamental ideas behind chakras are really not that difficult to understand. In the human body, there are seven primary energy centers in which energy is continually flowing. These centers are located all throughout the body. Each point is considered to have its own Chakra, and each point also has its own name: the Base, the Sacral, the Solar Plexus, the Heart, the Throat, and the Crown. However, we are not going to concentrate on these small energy nodes at this time. There are, of course, more minor energy nodes dispersed between these large places.

In spite of this, these seven primary energy centers are responsible for regulating the natural processes that occur inside our bodies. For instance, one Chakra is in charge of our immune system, another Chakra is in charge of our brain system, and yet another Chakra is in charge of the activities of our stomach and intestines. In a nutshell, each Chakra is accountable for the regulation of a distinct set of processes and systems located inside our body. Therefore, contrary to what people who aren't acquainted with the concept would imagine, chakras aren't only connected to people's mental moods. Each energy location does, of course, influence a distinct aspect of our mental makeup, such as our open-mindedness, acceptance, and optimism; but, each Chakra is also in charge of the physical processes that occur inside our bodies. It's really fascinating, isn't it? After all of this has been stated, the chakras develop into their very own system inside of our bodies. If one of the chakras is out of balance or even closed (both of which are occurrences that we will learn more about in the next chapters), then the Chakra system as a whole is at danger of being out of balance.

Chakras are inherently a part of spirituality; nevertheless, just because they are a part of spirituality does not imply that only spiritual people may accept them. Chakra-opening activities may be incorporated into the everyday lives of absolutely everyone, regardless of age, gender, religious affiliation, racial background, or spiritual orientation (you'll learn more about these exercises in the next chapters). Therefore, the easiest way to understand the Chakra system is to consider it to be the blueprint of your soul.

I really hope that you are not experiencing any feelings of being completely overwhelmed by all of this knowledge. In all honesty, chakras are quite straightforward concepts, at least when it comes to the fundamentals that will be covered in this book. I've devoted one chapter of this book to each of the seven chakras so that your journey of self-discovery may go with less friction and greater success. An introduction Chakra exercise will be provided at the beginning of each chapter. This activity will help you polish the abilities you'll need in order to get acquainted with each of the seven primary energy centers that are distributed throughout the body. After completing the warm-up activity, you will go on to the subsequent chapters, which will each provide you some background information on the

Chakra, including where it is situated and what it affects. After that, we will discuss how to identify an unbalanced Chakra and how to restore its proper function. The majority of chapters will wrap up by demonstrating how we may use what we've learned about chakras in our day-to-day lives. At the end of these sections, we'll typically be introduced to an extra chakra-activating practice that we can do at appropriate times.

In utero, organ development begins with the formation of the heart. It serves as the focal point of your body. The second chakra that most people forget about is the heart chakra. It is incredibly vital, yet people often disregard its significance. When you open your Third Eye chakra, you often find that your Heart chakra remains locked. Once you have the ability to see, you could be confronted with things that your heart is unable to process. The lock is triggered when it is damaged. This might cause problems in social situations or in relationships. The Heart chakra is quickly shut down by critical thinking. Grief, on the other hand, has a disproportionately negative effect on the Heart chakra. Your capacity for empathy is controlled by this chakra. Anyone who works in the medical industry or as a caregiver must understand the significance of this topic. Due to the fact that it has the greatest frequency associated with healing, this chakra is associated with the process.

If your Heart chakra is blocked, you could notice that you have a tendency to always help other people. Giving up all you own without expecting anything in return. Because of this, you will feel completely fatigued. When you learn how to open the Heart chakra, you will be able to strike a healthy balance between giving and receiving, and this will leave you feeling revitalized. When you have awakened your Heart chakra, you are linked to the whole world, and as a result, you will never feel alone again.

What kinds of mental and emotional roadblocks are preventing you from opening your heart chakra? Have you been injured in the past by a member of your family or by a partner who has come and gone? Spend some time just being with yourself and your heart. If you find that seeing it as a little being helps, then do that. What is it looking for? What does it appreciate most? Is there a sense that it is appreciated or that it is undervalued? Ask it questions that are straightforward, such as "what makes you happy" or "what do you have to tell me?" Recognize the issues that it has. Give it the feedback that you believe it needs the most. Take action in order to grant its requests. After you and it have arrived at a mutually satisfactory agreement, demonstrate your gratitude to it. When you have a stronger connection with your heart, you will also have a stronger connection with your soul. It absorbs every painful experience you've ever had in your life. You need to work on strengthening the connection you have with your heart.

You need to be able to communicate how you feel to others and be honest about it. Inundate your Heart chakra with the noises it needs to hear to become balanced. Binaural beats at 341.3 Hz, the bij mantra, Yam, the sound of blowing wind, and singing bowls are the sounds you hear. When it comes to opening your heart chakra, nothing beats drinking green tea and eating other foods that are green. Put on as much green as you can reasonably manage. I would go so far as to suggest that you adorn with it as much as is humanly possible to do so. This is of the utmost significance in your private space. Spend some time in the great outdoors, preferably somewhere green and breezy. One of the best ways to connect with other people and feel love in a less stressful manner is via the performance of acts of kindness that are completely at random. When folks are just getting started, this is a simple task for them. Visualizing yourself inhaling via your chest rather than your nose or mouth might provide immediate relief for your heart chakra. Massage is a great way to unwind and may also play a significant role in assisting you in opening your heart chakra.

Restoring Health To The Throat Chakra

If there is a blockage in this chakra, it may lead to mental anguish and even physical sickness. If your throat chakra is blocked, you may discover that it is difficult for you to swallow, and you may also experience a great deal of nervous tension as a result. You will learn how to reduce that tension and cleanse the chakra energy path by reading this section. (The year 2019 in Houston).

reciting chants – Even while you may be familiar with the concept of chanting, it's very likely that you've never really done it before. Chanting is similar to singing, except instead of singing a word with your lips completely closed, you sing it with your lips slightly parted so that a tingling sensation develops on your lips as you chant. This is an excellent practice for working on your third eye chakra as well as opening up your throat chakra, so give it a try if you want to do both!

You are permitted to use the phrase "Ohm," and only you may choose the pitch at which you sing the "Ohm" and the length of time that you hold your breath while singing it. First, give this a go. Take a deep breath in, and as you exhale, begin reciting the mantra. Repeating it will help you clean out that chakra, so be sure to do it as many times as you can. Incorporating the chant into the exhalation of the meditation practice is another way to make use of this practice.

You do not need to be a member of the choral group in order to take pleasure in this jubilant singing. select a song that you love singing and sing it ("Know your throat chakra and how to unlock its power", n.d.). All you have to do is select a melody that you enjoy singing. Make singing a regular part of your life since it allows the throat muscles to function, which helps get rid of the pain in the neck region. It also helps open up the chakra, which results in your pain levels decreasing and you beginning to feel more relaxed. This is effective for a number of different reasons. When you focus your attention on something as uplifting as music, your chakra is not disrupted by the uncertainties and fears that you are experiencing. If you give this method in addition to practicing mindfulness a go, you will be well on your way to making a full recovery.

Move Your Body – There is a fantastic practice that you can take to assist you in cleansing the throat chakra. You can find it here. Take a seat on a firm chair, and check that both of your feet are touching the ground and are grounded. After that, you will need to tilt your head to the side and put the index and middle fingers of your right hand on the left side of the top of your head while bending your head in the opposite direction. Take a long, deep breath in, and as you exhale, feel the air rising to the top of your head. At the same time, pull your chin as close to your chest as you can. You will get relief right away. Repeat this exercise as many times as you can.

There are several yoga positions that may assist in opening the throat chakra.

These are the kinds of postures that will come naturally to you during your first few weeks of yoga sessions, but you may also practice them on your own. It is important to be conscious that the way you breathe varies depending on the position you are doing. as the instructor tells you to inhale, make sure you do so, and as you move about while exhaling, make sure you are aware of how the two things are coming together. When practicing yoga, it is important to coordinate your motions with your breath so that you may reach body movements and postures that would not be possible without the practice.

Position with the legs up the wall

You will find that this is an excellent all-around workout that will assist you in opening up the throat chakra. You should lay down on a yoga mat or on a hard bed that is up against a wall because you need to lie as near as possible to the wall and move your legs upward so that they are parallel to the wall. If you don't have a yoga mat or a firm bed that is up against a wall, you may use a yoga blanket instead. You want your feet to be perpendicular to the wall and as flat as possible, as if you were standing on the ceiling directly above you. Your arms should be outstretched at your sides in a relaxed manner. Hold this posture for around ten breaths before releasing your hold and reclining down on the floor with your last exhale.

A traditional shoulder stand

Place your hands by your sides while you are lying completely flat on your back on your yoga mat. The body is hoisted into the air, and as it does so, the legs are brought up to meet it at a straight angle. Keep in mind that you should inhale, then move your legs while exhaling. Then, as you exhale, take your hands and place them under your body to support it, and elevate your torso. Maintain this posture for a few seconds before releasing your hold and letting your body naturally return to the lying-down position. Repeat this multiple times because each time you elevate the body, it creates an opportunity for new blood flow to the neck region, which in turn allows the muscles in the neck to relax. Do this as often as necessary.

The position of the supported fish stance

This is a straightforward stance, although it could make you feel awkward as first. You will get used to it, however, as you start to notice that the neck region is beginning to feel better. To create a block, roll up a towel into a log, then place it on top of the yoga mat. You should adjust your body such that the tops of your shoulder blades are resting on each side of the block. Then, slouch forward until your shoulders are just slightly raised off the floor. Allow your arms to hang down at your sides, and allow your head to sink down toward the floor behind you. Your neck will get the necessary amount of stretch to facilitate the opening of the chakra when you do this. Take approximately ten deep breaths in and out, and as you let the last one out, bring your body into a standing position, extend forward, and relax.

The advice given in this chapter ought to be able to assist you with one of the parts of your body that causes you the most difficulty on a regular basis. The neck is subjected to a significant amount of stress and strain in today's society. Exercises pertaining to the other chakras may be found in the chapters that follow this one.

The Power That Comes From Being Spiritual

You are not the sum of your ideas and convictions. Take it into consideration. What you thought to be true when you were younger has changed through time. Throughout the course of your life, you have gained a lot of new knowledge, and with each new understanding, your opinions and beliefs have either remade themselves or been replaced entirely. Despite everything, you continue to be you. Your fundamental nature has not changed in the least; in other words, you have not lost any of your essentiality. Therefore, the terror that you feel when a long-held belief is called into question is not a genuine emotion. You don't have to go through life always living in dread of anything. This is your ego speaking, and your ego is a problem because it will always bring you into difficulty. That is something that you have probably been told a number of times. Your ego is leading you down the road to your own demise.

You can do incredible things if you let go of your fears, if you let go of the impulse to control the circumstance, and if you let go of what you believe to be your own limits. Even if the only thing you did was the mental breakthrough of letting go and simply working through it, it is still a significant accomplishment. The self-assurance that comes with finishing what you started is invaluable. There are numerous instances in our life in which we are the ones who bring about our own anguish by just being stuck in a mental quagmire from which we are unable to free ourselves. But we are able to. Utilize the resources that are at your disposal.

Wisdom is something that resides inside a person. You're probably familiar with the sensation of having the hairs on the back of your arms rise up, right? That queasy sensation you get in your stomach whenever you find yourself in a precarious situation? Your body is continuously picking up cues from the environment around you, and it is continually making an effort to transmit these cues to you via the form of sensations and physical impressions. You eventually got to the point where you could ignore them completely. This is a terrible plan. There is a purpose behind these feelings that you are experiencing. You should make it a priority to pay attention to any words of wisdom that come to you from your higher self or even from your soul. They have far more insight than you have.

Your intellect is an excellent instrument for finding solutions to difficulties at work, as well as for arranging trips and events that you wish to participate in. Your intellect will serve you well under such circumstances. Discovering your interests, figuring out how to be more content in your career and in your life, and looking for creative inspiration are all activities that need you to listen to your inner voice and access the higher level of self-knowledge that you carry inside your body. When you use the incorrect instrument for the job, like your intellect to uncover your passion, it's something that can only be experienced; it can't be reasoned through. You end up becoming psychologically stuck because you're attempting to solve a problem that might easily be solved with the appropriate instrument.

If clarity is the state of mind, the lucidity that one experiences when they are in sync with the wisdom that they possess, then wisdom may be defined as the perceptive understanding that one needs in order to make a better choice.

Sometimes, whether it's late at night or very early in the morning, you're driving along a road that you've traveled a hundred times before, but this time there's fog all around you. In spite of the fact that you are acquainted with the surroundings and the turns in the road, you are unable to see them because a dense fog is obscuring your eyesight. This is a location that you are quite familiar with. You have no choice but to reduce your speed and approach each turn on the road with extreme care until the fog lifts and you are once again able to see properly. Your mental state will also get obscured by the fog that surrounds you. It may be a cerebral fog, it is possible that it will be a physical fog, and there may even be a spiritual fog there, all of which will make it tough to see your way through.

The following are a few of the solutions available to you in order to solve this problem. Drink plenty of water, get plenty of exercise, and sleep well. I know, how uninteresting is that? It would seem that we are being informed on a consistent basis that we need them.

Each and every one of these requirements enables you to maintain a vivid sense of aliveness and to be more present. Maintaining your physical fitness is a useful weapon to have in your armory.

The ability to think clearly is priceless. Mental fogs are annoying since they inhibit your creativity and cause you to make many erroneous assumptions. Consuming foods that are good for you plays a significant part in this. You may not comprehend the full extent of the harm that is caused by the use of processed foods. The advantages of preparing fresh meals and eating entire foods, such as fresh fruit and vegetables, lean meats, and healthy fats, cannot be overstated. Not to mention the incredible feeling you get when you succeed. The second aspect of this is unloading your stress onto other people. I'm sure you'll agree that it's far simpler to say than to do. It may be as easy as giving yourself a mental pep talk on your way to work to remind yourself that you are making a deliberate decision to let go of the tension, and from there, it will become about becoming a habit. The environment that surrounds us is not within our control. We only have control over our own responses and how we choose to respond to the circumstances that we find ourselves in. It is much simpler to be in the here and now when one makes an effort to improve themselves and concentrates on being the greatest version of themselves that they can be. Be present and attentive, and try not to worry about how anything else is being seen or understood by others. It is not necessary to strive for perfection. It's not something that's necessary for us. We have this idea that we want to achieve perfection. When you really stop to think about it, there is beauty to be found in the imperfections. If you don't take the time to pause, appreciate the experience for what it is, and appreciate the people around you for who they are, you will be losing out on something really extraordinary.

The last one, spiritual fog, often occurs at the same time that you begin to question the reasons for anything. It is a sign of spiritual fog when you find yourself asking questions like "why me?" or "why did this happen to me?" to the cosmos, your higher power, or whatever it is that you pray to.

Sometimes a spiritual leader or a mentor will tell me that everything will turn out precisely the way that it is intended to. When I am going through anything difficult, it is a concept like this that I find really reassuring to hear. To tell you the truth, it is a relief to realize that it is not necessary for me to feel regret about the decisions I took in the past since those decisions led me to the place I am now, and the place I am now is a place I can enjoy. Regret is capable of leading us astray. The reality is that everything that has happened to us throughout the course of our lives has had a role in shaping who we are and how we got here. The more appreciation you have for that fact, the simpler it will be for you to let go of regret, concern, and the strain of expectations. People are often saying that life is too short to spend it living in regret, isn't that right? However, it is more than simply a proverb. It is laden with profound significance.

Meditation is one technique that may be used to break through a spiritual haze. This book provides you with a few different meditation exercises, but you can find many more of them on YouTube, in music shops, and on search engines like Google. Meditation is an excellent method for cultivating awareness, and the improved mental acuity that you will get as a result of this practice will be of tremendous advantage to you. Affirmations of the positive are basic and straightforward methods. The process of retraining your thinking via the use of conscious thought is one technique to create more of what you want in your life. A extremely powerful and profound expression of one's own unique truth is "I am." Whatever words you decide to follow after I am, they will be the truth for you. Choose carefully and attentively, basing your decision on what rings true for you. Put them out there for the world and the cosmos to hear by writing them down and reading them loudly to yourself. Allow them the opportunity to express in a variety of different ways.

Light Therapy For The Healing Of The Chakras

The Light and the Chakras

Working with light and visualizing a brighter future are both essential components of chakra balance. You may do this by just picturing the light entering various chakras in your body as a type of meditation, or you can utilize real color therapy, such as lamps of varying colors or clothing of varying colors, to surround yourself with the energy needed to accomplish this.

The chakras have a favorable reaction to color therapy because, of all the methods of chakra balancing, colors are the ones that are closest to pure energy. This explains why color therapy works so effectively. The light that comes from the sun, moons, and stars is, as is common knowledge, the most unadulterated type of visible light. We have to make sure that we spend a lot of time in front of this light source if we want to seem as natural as possible. Because we are creatures made of energy in its most dense and tangible form, we have the ability to realign our chakras and return ourselves to a more refined frequency by making use of the colors that make up the spectrum.

If you choose to surround yourself with or mentally promote specific colors, you will actually be 'feeding' or protecting that chakra. This is because each chakra has its own color linked with it, and you will see that hue when you look at each chakra.

Utilizing Color Therapy in a Variety of Ways

Put on the color that has been selected for your outerwear.

Put on some clothing of the selected hue or tie a scarf of that color around the chakra of your choice.

While you are lying down, place a light scarf or another light material of the color of your choice over the chakra, meditate, and allow yourself to relax.

Imagine that the color you've picked is completely surrounding you and enveloping you.

Carry a crystal of the color of your choice with you and, over the course of the day, position it in front of you with its pointer pointing in your direction. Imagine that it is radiating that hue directly into the sensitive body you have!

The Various Colors That Represent the Chakras

Diamond of white color – This nearly dazzling, cleansing light is used for the crown chakra, and it energizes you while also raising your energy level to higher spiritual dimensions. It brings you closer to the divine.

The emerald green flame is a kind of therapeutic viridian light that is physiologically nourishing and utilized to cure the heart chakra as well as lower chakras.

The violet flame is associated with the sacral chakra as well as other chakras in the body that are located below the neck. It signifies the divine male and the divine feminine uniting together to cure both your emotions and your heart.

Infusing your aura with an unconditional sense of safety and protection, rose pink light is good for the healing of the inner child since it is most obviously related with the sacrum and the base chakras.

Rose pink light is also most clearly associated with the chakras.

Yellow, also known as sunshine yellow, is connected to our sacral, solar plexus, and heart chakras. This color is symbolic of Christ awareness as well as kindness, benevolence, and giving.

Gold light is a more stronger form of the sunny yellow beam; this hue is related instead with the full body as well as each chakra, and it is beneficial for producing serenity, eliminating tension, and establishing harmony. After putting in a lot of effort, this is a great way to wind down.

Through The Use Of Color Therapy, Your Chakras Will Be Strengthened And Rebalanced.

In a previous chapter, it was noted that chakras have a strong association with color. Because of this, Color Therapy, a method that develops and rebalances your seven energy centers, is of great help to the chakras. In the following stages, you will be taught how to use a color bath to realign and rebalance your chakras.

RESTORING THE BALANCE OF YOUR CHAKRAS WITH THE HELP OF A COLOR BATH

Let's get started by doing a color bath for your top chakra.

Exercise for the Crown Chakra:

To start, choose a comfortable sitting position. Take a long, deep breath in and exhale through your mouth after inhaling through your nose. Repeat this process three times. Now, visualize the white light of God and the love of the Universe swirling around you in a clockwise direction, beginning at your feet and rising up towards your head. This motion should begin at the base of your feet and end at the crown of your head. Imagine that a white light is travelling around you in a circular pattern three times, each time beginning at your feet and working its way progressively upwards to your head.

Imagine a wavy purple light moving around a little bit above your head; this is the location of your CROWN chakra. Imagine that this light is moving in a direction opposite to that of the clock. If you are getting the impression that this isn't quite correct, try visualizing the light moving in a clockwise direction instead. Do you find it simple to direct this light where you want it to go, or does it seem to be stuck or difficult to maneuver? If you feel as if it is "stuck," continue to see the light swirling in the direction that you have selected, whether it be clockwise or counterclockwise.

Now, in your mind's eye, see the purple light whirling downward, toward your feet, or in a clockwise direction. Imagine the violet light whirling downward toward your feet and then ascending once again. If the heavy or stuck sensation lingers after the purple light, this indicates that there is an imbalance in your chakra. Continue to do this every day; the more you perform this exercise, the more your crown chakra will open up, rebalance, and begin to move more easily as a result of your efforts.

Exercise for the Third Eye Chakra:

Let's move on to the third eye chakra, also known as the brow chakra, which is situated in the middle of your forehead. Your ability to access your intuition is located in the third eye chakra.

Let's start by visualizing an indigo-colored light that is either traveling in a clockwise or counter-clockwise pace, depending on whatever direction seems the simplest or most natural to you at this moment. Now envision it going until it becomes simpler to move more smoothly or clearly. This should become easier as you continue. Now, visualize the indigo light circling around your complete body in either a clockwise or counterclockwise pattern (depending on which direction you like), beginning at your head and working its way down to your feet before returning to its starting point.

THE ROOT CHAKRA, ALSO CALLED THE MULADHARA

This is the most fundamental support for the whole chakra system, and it may be found at the very base of the spine, just below the perineum. The root chakra is the energy center that is responsible for maintaining a person's physical, emotional, and mental health. It is located at the base of the spine. Pain in the lumbar region or the bones, varicose veins in the legs, hemorrhoids, and other conditions may be brought on by an obstruction or deficit in this chakra. There is a lack of self-confidence and/or fighting spirit, despair, carelessness, etc., when seen from a psychological point of view.

Meditation is necessary for realizing the enormous potential of the root chakra and developing self-confidence if one wants to achieve rebalancing of the chakra. In addition, physical activities are important, but only to the extent that they are not overdone. Healthy hobbies, such as gardening, are also important.

2. THE HOLY CHAKRA, ALSO KNOWN AS SVADHISHTHANA

The holy chakra is the energy center that is just below the navel and is associated with the element of water. It is the physical manifestation of the emotional and sexual power center. An excess of energy may cause someone to become overly emotional and develop a preoccupation with sexuality. Insufficiency of energy may result in impotence or a lower libido, as well as retreat, despair, a lack of openness, and a loss of zest for life. We may recognize gynecological and urinary ailments, as well as issues with rheumatism, digestion, colon, and other conditions, as being among the ills that are produced by an imbalance of Svadhishthana.

Meditation helps restore harmony to the holy chakra when it is practiced regularly. The procedure entails concentrating on its location, which is the region below the navel, and seeing an orange sphere around it. Orange is the hue associated with Svadhishthana. It is essential to maintain concentration on your breathing during the whole practice by taking full, slow breaths in and out at regular intervals. Ylang-ylang, Jasmine, Rose, Patchouli, Sandalwood, and Sage are some of the essential oils that are recommended above others.

3. THE SOLARCORE CHAKRA, ALSO CALLED THE MANIPURA

The solar plexus chakra is the energetic and emotional core of the body, and it may be found just below the point of the sternum. It is at the root of everyone's individuality and may be used to stimulate the healing of any and all kinds of illnesses. Aggression, the desire to dominate others, and the propensity to belittle oneself or others are all behaviors that may be attributed to having an excess of energy. A lack of energy may result in a loss of drive and ambition, as well as hesitation and other negative mental states. There are a variety of health issues that may arise as a result of blocked energy in the Manipura chakra, including but not limited to bulimia, anorexia, arthritis, intestinal illnesses, or respiratory difficulties.

During the meditation session, you need just to sit in a comfortable position and picture a golden ball in the middle of the solar plexus chakra. This is meant to warm the body. Cedar wood, cypress, elemi, ginger, mint, grapefruit, and Ylang-Ylang are some of the essential oils that you should prioritize using.

What are Mantras? is the topic of Chapter 5.

The word'man', which means to think in Sanskrit, is where the English word'mantra' originates from. A mantra may be a single word, a phrase, a poem, a prayer, a song, a charm, or an incantation. It can even be a whole prayer. Mantras are practiced with the intention of arriving at a state of righteousness. On both the material and the spiritual levels, mantras have a value that cannot be overstated. Because they are founded on energy, some sounds, when spoken in a certain manner and examined inside, may help one's woes go away and ensure one's redemption.

There are mantras in each and every faith and language. According to one of the hypotheses put out by the Eastern metaphysical tradition, the human body is made up of a mixture of five components, the first of which is sound. According to the findings of studies on the symbolism of sounds, vocal sounds have significance, regardless of whether or not we are conscious of that meaning, and there may be several levels of symbolic alliances associated with each sound. Therefore, even though we do not comprehend them, mantras do not lack meaning; there is no verbal utterance that is completely devoid of significance.

Altering one's state of awareness may be accomplished by meditating with the use of a mantra and reciting it over and over again, at first aloud and later in their minds. Mantras are sonic symbols, and their meaning and function are contingent upon the viewpoint and intelligence of the individual who repeatedly utters them. Many people believe that OM was the very first sound that existed in the cosmos. It is not necessary for a person to comprehend the meaning of a mantra in order for it to have any effect. Whether or not a person is aware of it, the sounds of one's own voice carry significance. The powers of mantras are mystical and have the potential to alter a person's state of awareness.

Let's pretend for a moment that someone has insulted us or made fun of us. How do you think you would react? What effect does it have on us? What does it give birth to? It irritates us, it generates bad vibrations; we get seething feelings in our stomach, a certain pain physically, our muscles tighten up, and we feel rigid in the brain and throughout the rest of our body.

When words that are critical of us may cause psychological and physiological responses in us, then repeating words that have good vibrations from the universe can really be beneficial to us on all levels. Positive vibrations are sparked inside us as we recite mantras, and the energy fields that surround our etheric bodies serve to protect us.

The enigmatic sound symbols known as mantras are used to call upon the energies of the spiritual realm. They often include phrases like Om and Ah Hum (which is pronounced as hoong), neither of which have any significance when spoken literally. They are different frequencies of sound. To attempt to intellectually understand the significance of chanting mantras is like to driving while wearing a blindfold on a busy highway.

The incessant internal chattering and disorder that are hallmarks of the monkey mind are quelled by reciting mantras, which also assist provide peace to the mind. It is possible to see things and the circumstances of one's life with an open mind and without passing judgment if one can keep their thoughts calm. The most of the time, we are not even aware that we are thinking.

The practice of mantras cultivates awareness and trains the intellect to be vigilant and to see things from a distance. This results in the least involvement possible and enables a person to detach from the drama that is generated by the mind. Chanting establishes a mental distance from habitual thought processes that are completely superfluous and progressively flushes away unwanted thought patterns, resulting in an empty, balanced, and serene state of mind.

Have you ever pondered the reason behind the sudden surge of energy you have when you see a specific person or go to a certain location? When you come into contact with good energy, this takes place. In a similar vein, there are certain individuals, some of whom you may not even know, who make you feel repulsed.

This takes place as a result of friction and an imbalance in the energy field around them. They are unable to generate their own good energy, so they draw it from others around them and their surroundings. As a result, folks who are in close proximity to these individuals report feeling depleted.

People like this are sometimes referred to as "psychic vampires." It is possible to ward off psychic vampires by maintaining a reservoir of good energy inside oneself and being concentrated within one's own consciousness. A positive person has the ability to influence the awareness of others around them, which in turn has the effect of bettering the surroundings. Those who have engaged in the practice of self-inquiry for an extended length of time, as well as saints and realized beings, are constantly surrounded by such an aura. Additionally, children exude an atmosphere of innocence.

It is recommended that you begin your practice of mantras and meditation by first chanting the mantra aloud. Doing so will prevent you from dozing off or allowing your mind to wander while you concentrate, both of which are common problems for beginners. Keep track of your breath and synchronize your chanting with your conscious inhalations and exhalations. While you are becoming more attuned to the methods, you may choose to repeat the mantras in your head by paying attention to your breathing.

What Exactly Are The Chakras?

Simply said, a chakra is the location at where the spirit and the physical body are connected to one another. The term "chakra" comes from a Sanskrit phrase that translates to "wheels of light." These "wheels of light" are the energy centers that are located throughout the human body. Each chakra has a certain function and is associated with a particular component of your body, mind, and spirit. One further way to think about chakras is as the portals through which awareness travels. Each of the chakras has a spiritual lesson that, when fully internalized, may pave the way to a more evolved state of awareness.

Because chakras are analogous to spinning wheels filled with unadulterated radiant light, both the pace at which they spin and the direction in which they spin are indicators of how well or open we are. Additionally, chakras perform the function of the body's antenna, picking up a vast range of energy information that you may or might not consciously be aware of or choose to make use of. You may be wondering why this is the case. The reason behind this is because the human body acts as an electric point through which waves and electric vibrations may travel. They react to the information that they are tuned to, which is sent to them by vibrations. The information is transmitted to them. They work on the same principle as a radio, which is that if the signal is not clear or not on the proper frequency, there will be static. Similarly, an out of tune chakra may create issues if it is used in a way that is not appropriate for it.

Additionally, chakras and auras function as transformers in the body. They connect different portions of the physical body to its non-physical counterparts and intercept energy with a vibrational frequency that is comparable to their own. If you allow any bad energy to enter the chakra, it will cause problems in your body, either psychologically, spiritually, or even physically in the form of an illness. This indicates that your chakras and auras have the potential to do severe harm to your body at times, and the only way to stop harmful energy from entering your chakras and auras is to ensure that they are in a state of harmonious equilibrium. You have to transfer the energy in your chakras in order to prevent it from having a detrimental effect on your life, which might even lead to your death.

The flow of mental, emotional, and spiritual energy into the body occurs via the chakras, which are also the doors through which this energy manifests physically. This simply means that they are the conduits via which your belief systems and attitudes flow into and shape the structure of your body and mind. Following its journey through the chakras, the energy that you generate as a result of your mental attitudes and the emotions you experience is then sent to your organs, tissues, and cells. You are now in a better position to comprehend how you influence your body, mind, and circumstances, and whether those effects are for the better or for the worse as a result of your newfound knowledge.

It is generally accepted that every person has seven basic chakras, which together comprise the human energy system. Each reflex region in your body is said to connect to a particular chakra. Let's take a look at each of these seven chakras in further detail.

But before we go into it, I want to acknowledge that the term "aura" could seem strange to you. Permit me to provide a quick explanation.

It appears as if everything around us is vibrating at an ever-changing rate. This occurs not just on the things that are visible to our naked eyes but also on those things that are invisible to them. For example, each and every atom, as well as each and every portion that makes up an atom, our thoughts, and even our own awareness, are all constantly vibrating. An aura is the electro-photonic vibration response that every item has when subjected to any external stimulation (light is one of the sources of the external excitation). This is why an aura is described as the electro-photonic vibration response.

This aura extends outward from your physical body at a distance of around three feet; however, some individuals have auras that are far larger than this; for example, survivors of rape or incest have auras that extend approximately fifty feet around them. What you understand to be your own space is the region that is inhabited by the aura. When someone is too near to you, you will often receive the impression that they are trying to invade your personal space or drain your vitality. The explanation for this is very straightforward: they are present inside your aura. Someone whose aura extends up to fifty feet would, then, incessantly have the impression that other people are invading their space even though those other individuals are quite a distance away.

A variety of colors may be seen emanating from living objects, including people in particular, depending on the state of both their physical body and their mental state. Simply put, this implies that our auras are our unique spiritual signatures, which we are unable to imitate even if we try. This, in turn, indicates that you are able to perceive someone's thoughts even before that person is able to verbalize them. In this situation, it is obvious when someone is trying to deceive you.

In this context, those who have a clear, brilliant aura are those who are spiritually enlightened and have good intents, and it does not matter whether or not these people are conscious of their aura. However, regardless of how articulate, well dressed, or well looking a person may seem to be, if they have a black or gray aura, it is safe to assume that they have bad intentions.

Now, let's shift our attention to the Chakras.

Practices For Opening And Balancing The Heart Chakra

Meditation on the Heart Chakra 1

Put yourself in a position where you can sit comfortably, either on the ground or on a chair with your feet firmly planted on the ground. Keep your posture correct by keeping your back straight without becoming tense. Put your hands on your lap with the palms facing up; this will help you be more ready to take what is being offered. You should take a few deep breaths, in through your nose and out through your mouth, and then gently shut your eyes. Examine your whole body in search of regions of stress, giving close attention to your chest region if you have any symptoms of tightness or constriction there. Continue to breathe into those regions until you can feel a release beginning to take place.

Focus your awareness on the heart chakra, which is located in the middle of your chest, when you are feeling calm and at ease. Visualize the air entering this chakra from your nose as you inhale, and the air leaving your body as you exhale moving back up your spine and out.

Imagine that your heart chakra is home to a beautiful green lotus flower with 12 petals that are all securely closed. As you breathe into your heart chakra, the lotus flower will start to light with each inhalation that you take. Its petals start to unfold with each inhalation that it takes. Keep directing your breath into your heart chakra until the lotus has completely opened up so that it can both take in and send forth love.

When your heart chakra has reached its full potential, you may start to repeat the seed sound YAM with each breath. As you continue to chant, a light that is the color of emerald starts to emanate from the lotus flower. When you take a breath in, the prana, or universal love, is carried by the air into your heart chakra, which then causes the light to become even more intense. When you exhale, the love in your heart chakra expands and extends forth, filling first your complete body and then the space surrounding you. This happens with each breath you take. Imagine that the light is now extending even farther, through your town, across your nation, and finally engulfing the whole planet with the light of cosmic love.

Continue with this rhythm of breathing and imagery until you feel the warmth of prana's love filling and issuing from your heart chakra, where it is being accepted and given in equal measure. Imagine that the green light is gently returning to your heart chakra, where it waits, ready to be transported again on the air of your breath, when you are ready to bring your meditation to a close. Do this by visualizing the light gradually fading away. Let go of the vision, and take several nice, deep breaths while you close your eyes. Move your fingers, toes, and neck from side to side while also wiggle your fingers and toes. Once you feel prepared, you should open your eyes and go back into the room.

Perform this meditation whenever you experience a blockage in the natural flow of love in your life.

Relationship Between Two People Based On Their Chakras

Each chakra has its own unique way of being articulated, and they each represent a distinct aspect of existence. When two individuals come together in any kind of relationship, there is also a chakra connection that is made between them. The energy comes from the right side of the chakra, and it is accepted on the left side. This is how the chakra may provide. When anything like this takes place, the stream will continue to be changed. Regardless of this, it's not absolutely necessary that the transmission be perfect all of the time. It is possible that there is a corresponding obstruction in at least one of the chakras. The great correspondence is exacerbated if the chakra of the sender is blocked, damaged, or either underactive or hyperactive. The blocking, damage, or activation of a chakra may be remedied by the use of chakra representation, recuperative practices, meditation, and breathing exercises that focus on chakras.

What a remarkable connection it creates between two individuals when their chakras correspond to one another:

The Sacral Chakra is the chakra that is associated with joy, originality, and self-assurance. In addition to that, it is associated with dread, a need for self-preservation, and an insatiable appetite. When a pair communicates via the sacral chakra, it results in an attachment that is susceptible to comfort and wealth. They will probably live a nice life, with a lovely house full of gorgeous furnishings, and a pristine and amazing automobile parked in front of their home. They need to work together in order to accomplish what they want.

This chakra is connected with the fundamental senses and is impacted by sexual energy. It is located at the base of the spine. The survival nature chakra is the one that provides the impetus to go on living. It also has a connection to one's conscience as well as their childlike nature. The pair who is aligned with their root chakra values the organization that each other brings to the relationship.

The Solar Plexus Chakra: This chakra is related to the energy chakras that are present in the light body. It is also compared to desires, goals, and material delights. These couples have autonomy from a young age and enjoy the opportunity to participate in games and competitions with one another. Accolade and prominence are both essential to their success.

The principal chakra beneath the larger quantity of energy focuses that inspire a healthy connection is the one located in the center of the chest, known as the heart chakra. These couples want to live together in happiness and tranquility, and they need such things for one another.

The Throat Chakra: Individuals whose beliefs are influenced by the throat chakra have a responsibility to develop their faculties. These two people are really religious. They find inner calm via meditative practices. They become more trustworthy and confident as time goes on. They need just give thought to developing their higher selves, which does not force them to rely on their natural sensations.

People who are associated with the third eye chakra engage in acts of self-acknowledgment on a regular basis. Their deep and meaningful connection compels them to sacrifice their life for the sake of the enjoyment of others. Their primary goal is to find contentment and tranquility. When they are together, they need to practice being faultless with one another and have a shared interest in learning about the universe. Their relationship is one that is more spiritual in nature as opposed to sexual.

The Crown Chakra The crown chakra is associated with a kind of love that is otherworldly and wonderful. These couples have absolutely no desire for sexual activity; having sex is just something that comes up naturally in the course of their relationship.

The "Anahata" Chakra Is Located In The Center Of The Heart.

This chakra is associated with the kinesthetic sensation of touch. It is situated close to the plexus of the heart and has an influence on an individual's sense of self-identity, as well as their capacity to impart knowledge and love that is unconditional, as well as their capacity for patience and comparison. When this chakra is out of alignment, it has a negative impact on the upper back and the shoulders, and it may also lead to heart and lung ailments, asthma, and other respiratory disorders. There are also mental and emotional problems that might surround a person who does not have this chakra in a balanced state. Some examples of these problems are a lack of empathy and compassion, wrath, anxiety, and even jealously. You have an empathetic sense, you are cheerful, and you are free of any animosity when this chakra is in a state of balance. Lavender and jasmine are two examples of essential oils that might help bring this chakra back into balance.

The heart chakra is the fourth chakra in the body. It causes the chakras to become disconnected from one another, and as a consequence, it often results in qualities that influence the individual's way of spirit. People that are defiant in this area are often reserved and lack empathy for others. They have a difficult time forgiving others, and as a result, they often feel angry and are unable to develop healthy ties with other people. This deficit may lead to a range of adverse impacts on a person's health, including difficulties with, among other things, the heart. High blood pressure, heart disease, and jealousy are all examples of disorders that are seen often. Backbends and the Eagle Pose are two of the suggested yoga positions for stimulating this chakra as part of your practice. Even while these things are helpful, the one that is most helpful and provides the most effective kind of rehabilitation is love, both the capacity to love and the ability to be loved.

The Anahata chakra is located in the middle of the chest and is responsible for regulating the functions of the lungs, blood, the circulatory system, the thymus, the diaphragm, the heart, the esophagus, the shoulders, the arms, the legs, and the breasts.

Compassion, forgiveness, passion, dedication, love for self and love for others, as well as your circulatory system, are all directly impacted by the heart chakra. If this chakra is out of balance, it may cause health problems such as lung cancer, pneumonia, breast cancer, shoulder difficulties, confidence issues, envy, fear, hatred, despair, confidence, passivity, and jealousy. Shoulder problems can also be caused by an imbalanced chest chakra.

Your energy is stored in the heart chakra, which is also known as the "heart of healing" and "the center of love." This energy area is linked to your emotions and gives you the ability to love and give without condition. In addition to this, it makes any necessary emotional healing easier to accomplish and acts as a link between your physical body and your spiritual self. When this chakra is activated and functioning properly, you will have a sense that you are linked to everyone in your life.

Solar Plexus Chakra: The Ability to Take Action

The name "Manipura" literally translates to "city of jewels" or "lustrous gem" in Sanskrit. The graphic representation of the solar plexus chakra is a circle with 10 petals around a triangle with its tip facing downward. Both the element of fire and the transforming force of the chakra are represented by the triangle. Yellow, similar to the hue of the flame, is the color that is most often used to depict the 10 petals.

This chakra is often found at the level of the solar plexus, which is defined as the region of the body that is between the lower half of the chest and the navel. Its primary function is to assist in the transformation of materials into energy that may be used by the body as fuel, and it also assists in the regulation of metabolism.

The energy point that controls our own strength and self-confidence is located in the solar plexus chakra. The manifestation of one's will, personality, sentiments, sensitivity, and mental talents are the defining characteristics of it. From this very spot, knowledge pours out into the world. Where do you get the sense that something isn't quite right or that things aren't going to go as planned in the circumstances in which you have a premonition that things won't go well? The overwhelming majority of individuals have what is known as a "gut feeling," which comes from the word "gut."

Although the solar plexus chakra is most often connected to the fire element, certain therapeutic approaches also relate it to the air element. It has a connection to all types of power, including the energy provided by the sun, heat, and light. The chakra has a golden appearance to it. Because it is connected to the quality of fire, it may also be shown as a color that is somewhere between yellow and reddish orange.

In order to restore equilibrium to the Solar Plexus chakra, we have to purge ourselves of any and all disappointments that lie deep inside us. We have to let go of our remorse and come to terms with the fact that our imperfections are an integral part of the complexity that makes us entire.

The Solar Plexus Chakra and Other Complementary and Alternative Treatments

Yellow is the color.

Fire is the element.

Position: Beginning at the middle of the navel and continuing all the way up to the breastbone (the point where the ribs meet).

Blockages may cause a variety of emotional conditions, including anxiety, nightmares, sleeplessness, eating disorders, inclinations toward jealousy or aggression, and a lack of sensation.

Heartburn, stomach troubles, and being overweight are examples of physical ailments that may result from blockages.

Yellow citrine, tiger's eye, rainbow fluorite, chrysoberyl, cat's eye, bronzite, amber, and yellow jasper are some of the crystals that may be used for healing.

Chamomile, fennel, and juniper are some of the herbs used for medicinal purposes.

The Bach Method of Healing Impatiens, Hornbeam, and Scleranthus are some of the flowers used in flower therapy.

Anise, chamomile, lavender, lemon, and myrrh are some of the essential oils that may be used for healing.

Using sound therapy, chant the "RAM" sound, which is the "universal seed sound."

Affirmations as a Healing Method: "I am successful in achieving every goal that I set, and I have faith in my decisions." "My inner fortitude leads the way for me to contribute to making this world a better place."

Activating the Chakra Located in the Solar Plexus: Put some yellow on your clothes. Listen to music that will put you in a romantic mood, talk about how you feel, and unwind in front of a fire or candles while taking slow, deep breaths into your stomach.

Position for Meditation and Yoga: the Plank

A Glance At The Contemporary World

These days, getting things done as quickly, laboriously, and as soon as possible is the most important thing. The issue with it is that a lot of folks are clueless about how to disconnect or take things more slowly. This is going to have really detrimental effects on us in the long run. We have never been more overweight, under more stress, or in worse health than we are right now. All of this is directly connected to the fact that we are not living healthy lifestyles and that we are unable to stay one step ahead of the curve in terms of our wellbeing. This indicates that we need to make the time to step away from the computer, as well as know when it is appropriate to do so and how to do so effectively. It should come as no surprise that many individuals do not have a healthy balance in their life given that the majority of us now spend more than 12 hours each day in front of a computer.

Numerous studies have conclusively shown that you will never be able to recuperate from the pressures of your week if you do not allow yourself some time to relax and include some sunshine into your daily routine. Do you feel that you are working all the time, even when you are supposed to be relaxing? Do you continually check your email and never take a break, despite the fact that you know this behavior is detrimental to your health? When you need to know is that you need to take some time for yourself, disconnect everything, and then charge your devices.

You need time to yourself in order to make sure that you are at your best and that you are able to recharge, much as your mobile phone needs to be connected into the wall in order to work properly. This ensures that you will have the greatest possible access to all of the materials that will assist you in achieving your goals and achieving success. You have to make sure that you schedule enough time for yourself to be able to disengage. You will be able to enjoy a more peaceful night's sleep and wake up feeling certain that your brain has been restored if you just do something as simple as turning off your mobile phone before bed. However, this implies that you should also make preparations to disconnect. When you get home from work, you should not immediately start hurriedly working on your emails. This would imply that you will not be able to get access to all of the resources that you need in order to be able to refocus and recuperate from the strains that you experienced during the week.

Finding the correct equilibrium in your life will ensure that you are successful over the long run and that you will have access to all you need in order to be successful and happy. Without the joy that comes from inside, none of the external luxuries in the world will ever be able to make up for the void left by your lack of contentment or aid you in regaining your equilibrium and maintaining your health. For this reason, it is up to you to identify the best possible strategy to take command of both your health and your future. This responsibility falls squarely on your shoulders. Find the optimal equilibrium that provides you with everything you need to be successful in life and it will be yours for the taking.

How To Awaken Your Dormant Root Chakras

You may open your chakra more effectively if you first practice grounding, which means you tie yourself to the earth. This is one of the most effective techniques to open your chakra. To do this, alter the distance between your feet so that they are shoulder-width apart and then shift your pelvis forward while bending your knees slightly. Maintaining your body's equilibrium will help you equally distribute your eight. After you've established a connection to the earth, you should sit with your legs crossed and gently attach your index finger to your thump.

Imagine the root chakra as a closed red flower with highly potent energy shining inside it. As you focus on this chakra, the flower opens up to reveal four petals that are each full with energy. Twenty to thirty minutes should be spent contracting, holding, and releasing the perineum breath. Your root chakra ought to become more open as a result of this.

A Guide to Opening the Sacral Chakra

Beginning by sitting on your knees with an upright posture and a straightened back is the first step in opening your second chakra. Place your hands on your lap and turn them so that the undersides of your palms are facing up. Your left hand should be positioned such that it is below your right hand when you use it to touch the rear fingers of your right hand. Join the palms of both hands together at the thumps. Put your attention on the chakra and the area of the body that it symbolizes, which is located below the navel. Chant the word

"VAM" in complete silence as you take slow, even breaths. You should continue doing this for at least half an hour or until you feel fully relaxed. This exercise will help you to cleanse your thoughts while also ensuring that the door to your sacral chakra is open.

The Solar Plexus Chakra: How to Open It

Maintain an upright position while sitting on your knees. Position your palm so that it is in front of the stomach, just below the upper belly, which is where the solar plexus chakra is situated. Put your thumps together, bring your fingers together, and then point them in the opposite direction of where you are standing. Pay attention to your chakra and the spot on your body where it is located. Chant the word "RAM" in a loud and clear voice as you keep thinking about the chakra, what it is, and what it signifies, especially how it impacts the many elements of life. Repeat this method till you are able to unwind and have a fresh feeling in your body.

How to Release Blockages and Open Your Heart Chakra

Take a seat and cross your legs in front of you. Join the tips of your index fingers in both hands to the sides of your thumbs. Put your left hand on your left knee, and your right hand should be placed just below your breastbone. Keep this posture for at least twenty minutes as you contemplate your heart chakra and its function in your body. Bring your attention to the middle of your chest and imagine what it is. While you focus your attention on your heart chakra and continue to relax, repeat the word "YAM" in your head quietly. Carry on with the exercise until you reach a point where you feel clean. After going through this procedure and opening your heart chakra, you will, after a few seconds of practice, experience a strong sensation of compassion for others.

How to Release Blockages and Open Your Throat Chakra

Once again, get down on your knees and start from there. Make a cross on the inside of each of your fingers, except the thumps. Put a connection between your thumps at the very top. At the level of the base of your neck, bring your attention to the throat chakra and what it stands for. Chant the word "HAM" in your head while keeping your focus on your throat chakra and how it relates to the rest of your life. Keep your voice low yet clear. If you do this for ten to fifteen minutes, you will experience a sense of calm and cleanliness throughout your body.

How to Awaken the Third Eye Chakra in Your Body

Put your legs across the seat. Put your hands in a position just below your breastbone. While you are touching the tops of their heads, point your middle finger away from you. Put your attention on the third eye chakra and the area of your body that it symbolizes, which is the middle of your eyes. Chant the word "AUM" or "OM" in your head quietly. As you continue to contemplate your chakra and the ways in which it influences your life, give your body permission to naturally relax. You should practice for at least twenty minutes, or until you feel clean, or until you feel stimulated to concentrate on your objectives and think of amazing ideas to attain them.

How to Activate Your Third Eye Chakra

Put your legs over your knees as you sit. Put your fingers together in a cross shape, with the exception of your tiny fingers, which should be brought together and touched at the top. Then, let your little fingers point upward and in the opposite direction away from you. It is recommended that the right thumb be positioned on top of the left thumb. Put your attention on the crown chakra and what it stands for, which is the very top of your head.

Your Own Internal Energy Structure

Now, we are aware that it is difficult to conceive of something that cannot be seen or x-rayed, much less come to a comprehension of what it is like. Now that we get that out of the way, let's talk about chakras and the level of understanding we currently have about this incredible system that exists inside us.

What what is a Chakra?

If you want, you may think of a chakra as an energy center that looks like a wheel and through which psychic and life force flows. Although they are analogous to acupuncture sites, chakras are not located somewhere in the body but have an effect on it. Instead, they are a component of your energy body, which is also often referred to as your spirit body or your subtle body. This is the same energy that provides life to your physical body and directs your intuitive thinking. There are many who believe that it is a component of your light body. In 1927, Charles W. Leadbeater put up a notion that has now gained widespread acceptance: that the chakras function via the electro-magnetic nature of our bodies. Because of this, chakras may be seen as electrical nodes or universal plug-in sites located throughout our bodies. (Leadbeater, 1927/2009) [Citation needed]

The primary chakras, which can be found in each part of your body in the region of your spine, work together to establish a communication and transit system for energy, not unlike to the way that the subway and railway systems in cities and nations function. The nadis, which are also known as energy channels, would serve as the lines along which prana (also known as light and energy) and information is transferred. The chakras would serve as the stations (sites of transfer and transformation).

There is a hue and a frequency connected with each chakra, as well as certain gemstones, plants, and even tarot card meanings. Because each chakra is related to the essential systems and organs of your body, it has the ability to influence all aspects of your being, including your mind, body, and emotions. The general position of a chakra as well as the color it is should be remembered as the two most important aspects of this energy center. Although all of these concepts may seem confusing at first. Easy!

Healthy chakras not only emit light and energy, but they also spin, which is why they are often referred to as wheels. The chakras are often seen in people's minds as luminous lotus flowers or pools of light. A number of individuals hold the opinion that chakras are not just energy vortices but also gateways to higher levels of spiritual being and experience. Do not let this frighten you in any way. There won't be any discussion about disappearing into an other realm here. All that we want to do is get a deeper understanding of chakras, including how they function, the impact they have on our well-being, and the steps we need to take to keep our minds, bodies, and spirits in good shape.

According to many spiritual traditions, our bodies are home to 88,000 chakras. To our good fortune, contemporary spiritual practices and energy workers focus their attention on the seven primary chakra points. These hubs are arranged in a manner that is parallel to your spinal cord, and they are positioned at nerve nexus locations. The first stop on our tour of the chakras will be the Root chakra, and from there, we will make our way all the way up to the Crown chakra. In this manner, we will go from the chakras linked with the physical world and survival to the chakras associated with the intellect and the spiritual world.

The first, or root, chakra

Because it serves as the starting point for the complete chakra system, we will begin with the first chakra center. This is an excellent location to begin! If you have not brought this specific chakra center into balance, there is a good likelihood that your other chakra centers are also out of whack. The seventh and lowest chakra center is called the Root chakra, which is fitting given that its primary function is to provide a sense of security and stability. This implies making you more aware of the environment around you by linking you to the Earth itself and making you feel more connected to it. Because you CANNOT correct the other chakras until you have first brought this one into balance, balancing it first is of the highest significance and should be done more than once. The location of the Root Chakra, which in Sanskrit is referred to as the Muladhara, lies at the very bottom of your spine, at the area in between your pelvis and your tailbone. The color red is associated with this chakra.

Your innate thoughts and actions are controlled by the Muladhara, which is located in the center of your brain. This is the source of the energy that drives the "fight or flight" impulse. The second facet of your existence that it controls is how your will is manifested in the world. The effort you put into obtaining that promotion, new home or vehicle, or even a new girlfriend is propelled by the energy that is present in this place. It is important to keep in mind that this is not the same thing as the strength of your will; rather, it is the expression or result of that force. Therefore, it would be to your advantage to concentrate on this chakra center if you are aware that you will soon be confronted with a challenging objective.

Therefore, in order to know how to repair it, you first need to know that it is broken, right? Now that we've got that out of the way, let's talk about a few things that can point to an imbalance in your Root chakra. Anxiety problems, being extremely scared, and having nightmares on a regular basis should be the first things to be looked for in a person who exhibits these symptoms.

There is a possibility that you may suffer none, some, or all of these symptoms, with the number of symptoms suggesting the likely severity of the internal imbalance. Problems with your colon, bladder, waste disposal, lower back, legs, or feet are some of the physical manifestations that might result when your root chakra is out of balance. Again, you may not feel all of them at the same time, but the fact that you can claim to have experienced at least three or more of them should serve as something of a warning to immediately begin balancing your Muladhara.

We are going to mention just a few of the many methods that you may enhance the health of your chakras, but this should be plenty to get you started. Spend some time investigating as many different strategies as you can while you're trying to get your chakras back into alignment. If you do this, you will increase the likelihood of discovering the strategies that are most suited to your personal abilities. Meditation is an effective method that may be used to heal the Muladhara chakra. Your meditation practice has the potential to act as a tool for anchoring you by bringing about a condition in which you are more aware of both your internal and external environments. Because the Muladhara chakra's sensory organ is the nose, bringing your attention to the tip of your nose as you meditate is an effective way to speed up the healing process for the Root chakra.

The Most Efficient Techniques To Rid Yourself Of The Sins And Bad Energies That Have Accumulated Through Time

First method: water has mystical properties.

You may ask why Christians and Muslims utilize water as a means of purification, and the answer is that there is a definitive rationale for this practice. What time did they finish? To become a Christian, the first step is baptism, which involves being submerged in water and having all of your sins washed away in the process. However, why water? And how can one explain it in scientific terms? The process of cleaning and purifying the energy points in your body raises the question of why these areas even need cleansing in the first place.

People get depressed or feel anxious or get to experience any kind of illness because the bad energy and blockages that have blocked you energy points completely cause you to become or feel ill. Well, in case you didn't know this, every sin and wrong thing you do creates a bad energy and blockages in your body above the energy points. Well, in case you didn't know this, I will tell you now. Therefore, water may cleanse, but it cannot purify you until you first complete an essential procedure, which is as follows:

stepping into the water with the genuine and sincere purpose of allowing it to cleanse your spirit

Nothing will take place if there is no aim behind it. People have a habit of taking showers every day without the proper purpose, which is why they end up not receiving the outcomes they desire. On the other hand, someone who wants to be baptized will have his intention set correctly and will be fully prepared to receive purification; as a result, when he gets himself dipped into the water, he will really be cleaned and cleansed.

Before beginning the act of prayer, Muslims are required to perform a ritual known as "Wudu," which entails washing their hands, faces, mouths, ears, heads, and feet. This is done in order to cleanse and purify their energy points before to praying. Have you noticed that they concentrate on cleaning the main points, beginning with the hands, which are connected and linked to all body parts, and ending it by washing the feet, which is where the negative energy leaves the body. In between, they wipe their heads, which is the important point where you get charged directly from the divine, god of the universe. Have you noticed this?

The following verse from the Quran emphasizes the need of water in regaining one's vitality:

[21:30] of the Surah Al-Anbya: (Have those who disbelieved not pondered that the heavens and the earth were a united entity, and that We separated them, and that We produced every living creature from water? Then they won't believe, will they?

This verse is an obvious indication that water awakens and brings life into everything from your soul to your energy points to your physical body. When speaking about your physical body, this verse explains pretty well the reason behind the importance of water for all body parts, from hair growth to metabolism boost and many other aspects that you can start searching for.

Concentrate on consuming a large quantity of water, and in addition to that, wash and purify with the purpose of being cleaned and purified throughout the body and energy points. If you wash your body parts only once, it will help, but you need to do it every day because, let's face it, we are humans, and we sin every day and do things that are wrong here and there, regardless of whether we planned to do them or not.

The Chakra Located In The Navel Region

Yellow is the color associated with the navel chakra, which is said to be related to one's sense of self-assurance. You may discover enormous confidence and improve your ability to cope with other people by working with this chakra. The energy that is necessary to succeed at the highest levels of a business environment may be obtained via the navel chakra. At the same time, it is of great assistance to those who operate best in collaboration with others. Your affable personality and self-assured viewpoints will help you stand out from the crowd more than ever before.

When you open the navel chakra, you get greater control over your emotions and you activate the dignity that is already inside you. As a result of your mind's capacity to link your present issue with previously stored knowledge in your memory, it may also help you make excellent decisions fast and improve your ability to appraise diverse circumstances. This is because of how your mind works. You will be able to study and analyze a wide variety of facts in a way that is much more convenient for you than it was before you gained this new level of self-assurance.

If the yellow chakra is not functioning properly, the exact reverse may take place. When it comes to testing your abilities, you won't be able to put your faith in your gut instincts, and you'll feel perpetually uneasy about the situation. Simple issues will present themselves to you as challenging inquiries, and you will have the impression that you are unable to filter through any confusing information that you get. You will be coerced into acting in a passive manner, rendering you unable to make judgments in a timely manner.

This might also lead to a lack of self-confidence as well as an inability to make a contribution that is relevant to the society or organization that you are a part of. Your professional life will become filled with failures, and you will suffer a significant reduction in your sense of self-worth as a result.

In a similar line, having a navel chakra that is overactive may cause you to behave in an overly aggressive and competitive manner. You will become aware of a "rush of blood" in all of your activities, which will pull you away from a state of serenity and tranquillity. Because you will continually be in a "high" state, your ability to make decisions will also be negatively impacted.

It will become extremely difficult for you to remain cool and evaluate any complicated issue for what it really is, and as a result, you will be driven to make decisions that are not best for you since you will be unable to accurately evaluate the facts.

You may open your navel chakra and get all of the advantages that come with doing so by using a few simple procedures. Place your hands on your knees and sit in this position with your back straight yet relaxed. Relax your hands and let them dangle at your sides while you read this sentence. Now, gently lift your hands over your head and place them in front of you, just below your navel, with the fingers of each hand pointing away from you. It is essential that you place your hand in this manner.

Hold your hands so that your fingers are touching each other and your thumbs are crossed. Begin to focus your attention on the navel chakra as well as the area of your spine located right above your navel. Chant "RAM" to make yourself feel more relaxed, and as you're doing so, think about the benefits of this chakra and how it may help you lead a more fulfilling life. Maintain this stance and clear your thoughts of anything else by focusing just on the task at hand. Maintain this posture until you get that "clean" sensation in your body.

It is recommended that you conduct exercises for your navel chakra on a regular basis, especially if you are a working person and especially if your day-to-day existence requires you to make important choices. Something like this is conceivable for higher-level CEOs, whose choices in day-to-day operations may either result in significant gains for the stakeholders in their companies or in catastrophic losses for those stakeholders.

Crown Chakra Basics

The Crown chakra is the seventh and final energy center in our major chakra system. It also holds the most energy. It has to do with one's unadulterated awareness and their connection to a heavenly spiritual source, and it resides at the very pinnacle or just above it. Because this chakra is characterized as a lotus with 1,000 petals arrayed in 20 levels of 50 petals each, its Sanskrit name is Sahasrara, which means "thousand fold." This chakra is located at the crown of the head. There is a degree of overlap between this chakra and the Third Eye chakra due to the fact that the Crown chakra is also responsible for regulating the pituitary and pineal glands. In addition to this, it has control over the hypothalamus as well as the rest of the brain and skull. The color violet is the one that corresponds to it the most, however it may also be represented by a completely white hue. Ng is the bija mantra for the Crown chakra, and it should be spoken exactly as it seems, from the very back of the throat.

A Crown Chakra that is in Good Health

When this chakra is working properly, our brains are clear, and we experience a profound feeling of understanding that comes from inside. We have a sense of connection to the spiritual worlds and an awareness that all things are interconnected. When the energy in our Crown chakra is under check, we are able to communicate effectively with the rest of the cosmos.

Hydrotherapeutic methods and procedures

A whole or partial bath may be used in hydrotherapy to warm up or refresh the body. Sponging, compresses, and tablets are all used in this treatment method. Hydrotherapy is particularly beneficial against restricted diseases, but it can also be used as a replacement to baths when these are not feasible. Clay, hay, and linseed are some examples of the medicinal materials that are used on occasion in this process.

Orally, in the form of a drink; rectally, in the form of an enteroclisma or enema; for external use with clutches; with ablutions; in each of these applications, the user may be carried out partly or completely. The usage is expanded to include immersion baths, which may either be whole or partial, hot or cold, with or without the addition of herbal decoctions or infusions.

Baths of varying temperatures are used in a unique therapy that involves the patient immersing their bodies first into hot water and then into cold water. This provides the blood vessels with a genuine vascular workout. Lie-down baths, also known as sitz baths, are an alternative method of treatment for gastrointestinal issues, back discomfort, hemorrhoids, constipation, and urinary difficulties. Sitz baths include submerging oneself in a pool of water that comes up to one's hips.

The heat relaxes the muscles, loosens the joints, and provides relief from pain and discomfort. It also helps to improve circulation, which is facilitated by the dilation of the blood vessels. The cold constricts the blood vessels, which in turn reduces the amount of swelling and inflammation. In addition, it may bring down a temperature and serve as a local anesthetic.

The use of cold water has a decongesting effect on the region where it is applied if the area is small; however, if it is applied all over the body, it has a tonic action on the nervous system and stimulator on the circulatory blood vessel system; in this way, the blood flows more deeply into the skin tissue, causing overheating of the entire body surface; it opens the pores from which certain substances of the organic residue are freed from exhalation, frequently kept in the body; and

The Value Of Restoring Balance To Your Chakras

We are nourished and restored by universal energy, just as we are by food, drink, and air. The movement of energy into and out of our physical bodies is regulated and facilitated by the chakras, which are the organs that make up our energy centers. The chakras are responsible for bringing in new energy, which feeds our glands and organs and assists us in efficiently processing the events that occur in our lives. This results in psychological and emotional equilibrium as well as physical vigor.

Each of the seven chakras has a unique set of glands, organs, and aspects of life that are associated with it. When suppressed, emotional, physical, and psychological trauma may clog a chakra with bad energy and obstruct the free passage of good energy. This can happen whether the trauma was experienced physically or psychologically. Our capacity to process ideas and feelings associated with the blocked chakra is hindered when there is an imbalance in the flow of energy.

The accumulation of problems that have not been resolved may lead to a variety of negative outcomes, including physical disease, dread, doubt, sadness, anxiety, and destructive conduct. Lower back discomfort, skin illnesses, reproductive abnormalities, headaches, and respiratory and heart difficulties are some of the most frequent maladies that are related with misaligned chakras. In addition to these, other indications of an uneven chakra system include addictions, eating disorders, jealousy, and hesitation. When our chakras are in harmony, we are able to attain mental concentration and improve our immune systems, which in turn helps us avoid sickness.

Through the process of opening, purifying, and balancing our chakras, we make it possible for ourselves to absorb knowledge from the depths of our subconscious as well as the vastness of the cosmos. This knowledge is crucial to our capacity to repair the emotional, bodily, and spiritual issues that we are currently experiencing. Our capacity to let go of destructive patterns of behavior and change our vulnerabilities into strengths is enhanced by the healing energy that circulates through chakras that are in a healthy state when we experience an increase in our love for life.

When we become aware of our capabilities, our perception of who we really are becomes more stable, and we develop the self-assurance necessary to deal with unpredictability. We bestow upon ourselves the ability to dispel uncertainty with self-assurance and to replace monotony with originality. We also make it possible for ourselves to replace feelings of regret and dread with the capacity to fully appreciate the moment that we are in right now.

This awareness of one's own self-worth leads to improvements in all element of one's life, from relationships to economics, and bestows upon one the capacity to bring one's aspirations into reality. Our route through life gets more transparent, and it becomes less difficult for us to make choices. Our beliefs grow more solid, and we are hit with a deluge of inspiration that serves as a source of motivation for us as we work toward realizing our highest potential for good. When our chakras are in a state of harmony, we open up channels to an unending supply of universal energy. When we reach a level of consciousness and mental calm, we are able to respond to any kind of challenge with the self-assurance and ease that comes naturally.

Chakras are energy centers in the body that may be opened, cleansed, and brought into balance by anybody. You may access your inner knowledge and willpower by beginning with the simple and powerful chanting method that is detailed in this book. As a result, your personal integrity will increase, and you will be better able to set yourself on the road toward the satisfying life that you deserve.

Manifestations Of An Unbalanced Sacral Chakra And Its Symptoms

Experiencing low back discomfort, hip pain, or pelvic pain are all symptoms of an energetic imbalance in your Sacral Chakra. In addition to that, it may entail difficulties with sexuality and reproduction, dysfunctions of the kidneys, and urinary troubles.

Concerns of betrayal and a lack of creative expression are all symptoms of an emotional imbalance, as are difficulties in expressing emotions, having fun, having obligations in your relationships, and having problems having fun. You may also be dealing with problems related to your sexuality and the pleasure you get from it, such as anxiety over impotence or addictions.

It's also possible that you're shy, that you struggle with trust and connection, that your emotions are all over the place, and that you're too sensitive. If your Sacral Chakra is not functioning properly, you may find yourself acting needy, as well as cold and distant towards other people. Your fundamental emotional center is located in your sacral chakra, and virtually all of us, at some point in our lives, have struggled with an imbalance in this chakra.

How to Bring Your Sacral Chakra Back Into Balance

Your imagination will rise, you will be enthusiastic and extroverted, and you won't have any trouble taking chances when your Sacral Chakra is in harmony. You will have compassion, a grounded perspective, and an intuitive nature. You will have an open mind and be responsive to the things going on in the world. You will have a lot of energy, you will feel emotionally stable, you will be sexually stimulated, and you will have a lot of enthusiasm for life.

Now is the Time to Consider Orange

Imagine that your lower belly is being bathed in a soothing orange light that fills every available area. Send your breath together with the color orange to any part of your body that hurts, is tense, or is afflicted with a disease.

Don't You Want It?

Simply let go of all of those bad thoughts and memories, as well as the unhealthy individuals that have crossed your life, and turn them over to the cosmos. Instead of filling your space with unfavorable thoughts and feelings, it is much more vital for you to make room and energy for new and improved possibilities in your life. If you do not let go of this baggage, you will not have the room in your life necessary to make room for new vitality and prospects.

You will feel emotionally cut off from the world. Acquire the skill of trusting your own intuition, but do not give in to the temptation of letting your feelings control you. It is very normal for this not to come readily to you. It requires a lot of practice.

Time for yoga

Your hips are a storehouse for both the physical and mental strain that you carry. Because of this direct connection to the Sacral Chakra, yoga poses that focus on opening up the hips may be quite helpful to practitioners.

Are you still not persuaded? When you find yourself in a stressful situation, you should begin to become aware of the muscles that you tense up and clench. Your emotional centers are most likely located in the region of your neck, in your lower belly, and in your hips. These are the three most common locations.

Your hips may move in a number of different ways. Perform at least a couple positions in which you move your hips through their whole range of motion. Start by holding a single stance and concentrating on entirely letting go of your grip on the pose. The cow position (shown on the left) coupled with the cat pose (seen on the right) is a common combination.

Symptoms Of A Disrupted Energy Balance In The Heart Chakra

If your Heart Chakra is out of balance, you may find it challenging to form partnerships that are both long-lasting and significant. Both having intimate relationships with other people and connecting with them on the most fundamental level will be challenging.

You could also be weak in empathy and compassion, which causes you to have a pessimistic outlook on life and perhaps feel hatred toward other people.

If you lack compassion, it will be difficult for you to comprehend the fact that other people have the freedom to make decisions with which you may not agree and that those decisions are theirs to make, not yours to make. In light of these facts, it is quite simple to lack compassion and slip into a judgemental mindset.

What Kinds of Health Problems Can Result from an Unbalanced Heart Chakra?

Because it most often takes the form of a physical issue rather than a psychological one, this sort of imbalance is perhaps the most detrimental one that a person may have. Even breast cancer and heart illness have sometimes been connected to imbalances in the Heart Chakra; however, these are not diseases that can be remedied by drinking the appropriate colored drink or taking a warm bath.

Instabilities in this area may also create chest aches and difficulty in breathing, both of which are concerns that you would like to avoid having to deal with if at all possible. Even while no one completely comprehends the mechanism behind the potent impacts of the heart chakra, there is a great deal of evidence to show that this is the case.

Understanding Chakras

It is essential for you to comprehend the purpose behind the existence of the chakras inside your body in order to comprehend the influence that they have on both your mental and your physical well-being. You will learn a little bit about the flow of energy as well as some facts on the history of the chakras in this chapter.

The movement of vitality throughout your body.

You would have read the term "energy" quite a few times in only a few pages by this point in the book, and you would be wondering what I meant when I referred to the flow of energy. A common misconception is that the only shape that the various things in the cosmos may take is a physical one. This is the part where a lot of folks do it wrong. It's possible that you, too, have been led astray to believe in this way. Therefore, let us begin with the fundamentals. Do you recall a time when you were in school studying courses like Physics and Biology and being taught that everything is always made out of energy? Do you remember that? Have you also gained an understanding of the reality that every occurrence in the universe is composed of some kind of material? So, tell me about your conception of the material world. You would also have been informed about matter, which is a collection of molecules of varying sorts, as you would have been taught. If you remember anything about chemistry, you should know that each molecule is composed of protons and electrons, which bump against each other in order to produce energy. This is something you should have learned in school. This is the manner in which the energy may be discovered across the cosmos in each and every creature, regardless of whether or not they are alive. This energy may be found everywhere in your body, but it most often manifests as the electromagnetic energy that encircles your whole body and permeates every crevice. This energy, which is also referred to as the subtle energy, moves in a continuous cycle via the chakras that are located in your body.

You were just informed that there are seven main chakras located throughout your body, but there are also numerous lesser chakras that are necessary for your survival. While the main chakras are represented by your brain, the smaller chakras are made up of the nerves that run throughout your body.

Due to the fact that these chakras are connected to all of the glands in your body, it is imperative that you maintain the proper balance in them. These chakras work together to guarantee that you are content with the way you are living at all times. These chakras will purge your body of any and all pessimism, even the tiniest particle that may be there. In order to ensure your safety, they also protect you from experiencing any kind of injury, whether it be mental or physical. Because of this, it is very necessary for you to pay special attention to these chakras and make sure that they are always clean and in a state of balance. You will be able to protect yourself from harm only if you are able to preserve the appropriate level of balance at all times. In the next chapters, you are going to learn the best strategies for maintaining your own happiness at all times, so stay tuned for them!

The Seven Chakras And The Functions Relating To Each Of Them

Westerners are primarily acquainted with the chakra system that consists of seven chakras. Having said that, there is just one chakra system, which is something that even a newbie should be aware of. While some systems identify hundreds of main chakras, some only identify five of them. Each of these approaches to philosophy and spirituality has its own unique insights to offer, yet none of them are inherently flawed.

Both the alternative system and the system that lists many extra centers contain the five chakras in both the seven chakra system and the system that lists many other centers. This is comparable to stating that the body consists of five primary systems: the brain, the throat, the lungs, the stomach, and the liver.

All of the items on the list play a significant role in the way the body functions. We may make that number seven by including the eyes and the reproductive system. However, even if we broke the body down into its component cells, this would still only be a tiny fraction of the intricate biological machine that is the human body. This intricate machine consists of several nerve centers, bones, joints, blood arteries, intestines, and a great many other parts and components.

However, if you are instructing a youngster or a medical student who is just starting out about the many parts of the body, you do not begin by bombarding the student with list after list of the Latin names for the various bodily parts. On the other hand, you start with the main systems and how they function. Similarly, this is also the case while learning about the chakras. When we concentrate on the seven-chakra system, we are able to get a clear understanding of the locations of the chakras as well as the primary roles that each of them plays. As soon as they are mastered, it is simple to go to systems that are more complicated or provide alternatives.

Imagine that you are sat on a resilient surface, like a yoga mat or a gym mat, in either the lotus position or cross-legged posture. This will help you comprehend how these seven chakras connect to the different parts of the body.

Your Root Chakra is located at the base of your spine, at the portion of your body that is in touch with whatever you are sitting or standing on. It symbolizes the pillars upon which your existence is built, including the provision of food, housing, and money — in other words, all that is necessary for maintaining one's physical health. If you are in a standing stance, it establishes a connection with the nerves, bone, and tissue that enable you to walk erect, or, to put it another way, that "roots" you to the soil.

The next chakra is the sacral one. Although it is situated in the middle of the abdomen, it has some similarities to the reproductive organs and functions in a similar way. Relationships, emotional steadiness, a feeling of completion, and levels of joy and happiness are all controlled by it. When you think of the function of the Sacral Chakra, the phrase "gut feeling" often comes to mind. It refers to our most fundamental, id-driven, intuitive responses to the environment that we find ourselves in.

The Solar Plexus Chakra is in charge of directing both of these subordinate spheres. Our capacity to lead and arrange our life, as well as our capacity to think things through, is governed by this skill. It is the center of our sentiments of self-esteem and self-worth, as well as our overall perspective of the world.

The next chakra is the heart chakra, which, like the three chakras that came before it, is responsible for managing and directing energy. Here is the seat of our capacity to love, to establish connections that endure, to get passionate about problems, and unfortunately, the seat of our rage, hatred, and resentment, which are there right along with the wonderful emotions that are present.

It should come as no surprise that the Throat Chakra is concerned with communication, self-expression, and the expressing of sentiments to the outside world. Its activities are not quite as complex as those of the heart, but they are very necessary – very much like the nerves and blood arteries that are positioned in the neck and that bring messages and blood to the brain.

The pituitary gland is associated with the Third Eye Chakra, often known as the brow Chakra. The third eye chakra is responsible for governing comparable spiritual reactions, much to how the pituitary gland is responsible for the secretion of hormones that regulate many of our body's activities. It is our capacity to understand how the many components fit together. Some people think that it enables us to see things like auras, ghosts, and psychic imprints that have been implanted in objects. Others think that it only gives us the ability to view these things. Between the lower functions and the higher functions, it works as a gatekeeper.

In some ways, the Crown Chakra is analogous to the pineal gland, which is another essential component of our endocrine system. On the other hand, the Crown Chakra is analogous to the impact of Higher Beings. Consider your atheism to be the facet of your worldview that most strongly supports the idea that human flourishing is the most important thing in the universe.

In our etheric envelope, the seven chakras are the primary or major energy centers or systems. You may also think of them as a mnemonic device for the physical systems that make up our bodies. Either style of thinking will function well; the important thing is to choose a strategy for consideration, one that you can live with and put into practice. The Eastern ideologies as well as the Hindu practices include the chakras into their systems.

However, similar to the practice of yoga, you are not need to subscribe to those points of view in order to make use of the chakras as a tool to enhance your mental and emotional steadiness in addition to your bodily well-being. The system is not constrained by any one religion and collaborates directly with us in our natural state.

You may find it helpful to buy a coloring book that contains images of each of the main chakras as you go through the different chakras. One suggestion for finding such a book is online.

The First Chakra in the Body

The Root Chakra, also known as the Base Chakra, is the first of the seven chakras and may be found near the base of the spine. It is physically located somewhere along the portion of the tailbone that is placed between the anal exit and the genital organ. This area is known as the perineum. The Root Chakra, which is also referred to as the Muladhara Chakra, is the center of support. It is a symbol of the basis upon which a person is built.

There is a connection between the Root chakra and three different nadis. Ida, Pingala, and Sushumna are the names of these three. These nadis have their beginning in the Root Chakra, and they are responsible for transporting both the vital energy (known as prana shako) and the mental power (known as manas shako) throughout the body.

Everything that has to do with sustaining one's life is the domain of the Root Chakra. Because it provides you with the sensation of being rooted in the earth, it has a connection to the planet Earth. It controls sexuality, stability, sensuality, and a feeling of safety in addition to governing sexuality.

Emotional concerns relating to one's ability to endure are those that are associated with this chakra. It is concerned with issues relating to work security, financial stability, and the capacity to make a livelihood for oneself. You are experiencing issues with your Root chakra if you find that you are always questioning whether you have enough money to purchase food, pay the rent, or spend it on anything you need. When you are concerned about whether or not you have the support of family and friends, the same thing may be stated. However, you need to have an understanding of the true source of the assistance. It is derived from the planet itself. In order to become grounded and to free yourself from anxiety over your safety and ability to survive, you must maintain a clean first chakra.

Fear, bewilderment, and worry are the results of an unbalanced or blocked Root chakra, which you might manifest if you do not clear it. It is also possible for it to manifest as feelings of abandonment, melancholy, or hopelessness. Another symptom of a blocked Muladhara is fear, namely fear of one's own safety or the sensation that one is in danger. On a physical level, it could manifest as a lack of energy, discomfort, impotence, and medical concerns relating to the skin. It might also cause impotence.

dread prevents Muladhara from functioning properly; more particularly, the dread of not being safe or of lacking the resources necessary to continue living. You are anxious about your own ability to live. To activate this chakra, you must first identify the thing that scares you the most. You need to find out your worries in the same way that Guru Pathik instructed Aang to do. You have to have a better understanding of your worries. You have no choice but to let go of those worries and watch them go down the brook. Put aside your worries and have faith that you can triumph over any obstacle standing in the way of your safety and wellbeing.

You need to direct your attention to the spot where your Base Chakra is situated in order to assist cleanse it. Take a seat and try some meditation. You should close your eyes and picture a ball of energy radiating from your perineum or tailbone. Imagine for a moment suppose the ball was colored crimson. It is the hue of the Shakti, and it represents coming into one's own. The color red best represents the earth. It is a symbol of the abundance that exists on our planet.

You may chant the sound "LAM" and repeat an affirmation while you are meditating on the Root chakra and envisioning that ball of fire that is red in color. Repeat the following phrase as often as possible: "I am rooted. I have backing in this."

In addition to the practice of meditation, you might also engage in physical activities such as jogging, running, or yoga. Because they bring your attention to the body, physical activities of any kind help you become more self-aware, which in turn helps cleanse the Root chakra.

People often fail to appreciate the significance of the ground they walk on. They fail to understand its significance the vast majority of the time. On the other hand, if the Earth were to disappear, everyone would drift aimlessly across space. In order to clear your Root Chakra, you must first establish a connection with the earth. Stomping your feet may work wonders for unblocking your chakra, and it's a simple motion that everyone can perform. In addition to that, you may try this easy exercise:

Maintain a calm and upright stance with your feet at about shoulder-width apart. Before you move your pelvis forward, be sure that your knees are slightly bent. This might be challenging, so make sure you don't lose your equilibrium. Make sure that the soles of both feet are bearing an equal amount of your weight. Then move your weight to the front of your body. Maintain this stance for a few minutes as you gain a sense of the earth under your feet.

This Is The Throat Chakra.

The fifth chakra may be found at the junction of the collarbone and the base of the neck. It is also known as the solar plexus chakra. It is blue in color and has to do with expressing oneself honestly, accepting responsibility for one's own requirements, and establishing one's own personal power. It embodies our means of communication, the synthesis of sounds, our capacity for self-expression, and our aspiration to both say and hear the truth. This chakra is represented as a circle contained inside a descending triangle, and the sapphire serves as its gemstone. Saturn is its planetary home, and hearing is the sense that is most closely linked with it. The solar plexus chakra functions as the spiral pair of the throat chakra.

If you have an open throat chakra, you will have little trouble expressing yourself, and this self-expression may often take the form of creative endeavors. those who have a lot of surplus energy in their throat chakra have a tendency to be more stubborn, judgemental, and authoritarian. On the other side, those who have a lack of openness in their throat chakra have a hard time expressing themselves clearly, do not talk much, and lack faith. They also have a tendency to be shy, and presumably have an introverted personality, and they have difficulty expressing their opinions for fear of being judged. When your throat chakra is in harmony, you will have feelings of creative and even musical inspiration, and you will also have excellent public speaking skills.

A blocked throat chakra is linked to a number of physical ailments, including back discomfort, inflammations, sore throats, ear infections, skin irritations, and hyperthyroidism. The neck, the teeth, the ears, and the thyroid gland are all associated with the throat chakra because of their proximity to the area. In general, the throat chakra is at the core of our capacity to speak and express ourselves, not to mention the fact that it is the location where the inner voice of one's truth is spoken. Numerous people refer to it as the chakra of diplomatic communication.

Having Firsthand Experience With The Strength Of Love

The Anahat Chakra, also known as the Heart Chakra, helps us transcend our feeling of "Me, My, and Mine" by nourishing our hearts with love. When we are able to open our heart chakra, we are able to have more meaningful connections with the people in our lives. We are allowed to communicate our concerns and feelings to one another. When other people really understand and care about us, it makes us joyful. We are now more open to the perspectives of other people and more understanding of the limits they have.

Our feeling of freedom is diminished when we try to meet the standards set by the people we care about. We all place a high value on our independence and strive to further our knowledge by making our own blunders as we pursue this goal. On the other hand, even when we make quick advances toward development on the route we've chosen, we unconsciously put our expectations on the people we care about the most. There is not the slightest shadow of a doubt in anyone's mind that we love our friends and family very much. Nevertheless, we are unable or reluctant to "Let Go." Love is synonymous with liberty. Love requires making sacrifices. To love someone is to accept them just the way they are. Love is a state of inner calm, contentment, and harmony. And in order to achieve this condition of emotional equilibrium, we need to learn to 'forgive' and 'let go' of not just other people, but also our own pasts. This will need us to open the heart chakra.

Every time we are presented with a new obstacle—which is usually on a daily basis—we have the goal of achieving this sort of equilibrium. This internal conflict is what forces us to face and triumph over the unfavorable aspects of our personalities. We have come to the conclusion that we are the cause of our own suffering because we are unwilling to acknowledge the truth and would rather cling to the obsolete ideas and beliefs that we have. We must first make the effort to alter ourselves before we can even consider attempting to alter another human being.

Beneficial Activities: Reciting prayers, reading literature that provide inspiration, and lending a helping hand to those who are less fortunate than we are all assist to fill our hearts with compassion, patience, clarity, and love. These are the most straightforward and efficient methods for releasing any restrictions on the natural flow of prana via the heart chakra.

Exercises that focus on breathing may assist us in taming unruly emotions and coming to terms with them. If you do them on a consistent basis, you will see a greater improvement.

The word "YAM" is the mantra that corresponds to this chakra. By repeating this phrase, we are able to rid ourselves of our possessive impulses and understand what it is to "let go." We are able to access the wellspring of love that is inside our hearts by reciting the mantra SO HAM. We acquire the ability to forgive and to forget.

Green is the hue that is often connected with the heart chakra. Crystals such as emeralds, jade, peridots, and rubies are all excellent choices for clearing and healing work with this chakra.

Meditation is the most effective method for clearing up this chakra. We will progressively learn how to concentrate all of your attention on the wonderful experiences that we have had in the past during the meditation sessions. Because of this, we are better able to tap into the flow of energy.

When we focus the positive energy that we feel from these recollections on a particular loved one, we are able to strengthen the connection that we have with that person. As we investigate our history, we run the risk of reliving all of the heartache and disappointment we've been through in the past. The strength to face, triumph over, and ultimately 'let go of' these demons will be bestowed to us as we recite the mantra and say our prayers during the whole process.

The sequence of flowing asanas known as khatupranam is designed to act primarily on the anahat chakra. It also contributes to the balancing and harmonizing of the body, mind, and soul.

Activating And Deactivating Your Chakras

Before you make an effort to open your Chakras, it is important to have a fundamental understanding of the Chakras and the colors that are associated with them. Acquiring knowledge of the seven colors, in order from the root to the crown, will enable you to open or close your energy centers without drawing your attention away from the process by reading a list of instructions.

When opening and shutting your Chakra points, it is essential to make use of mental imagery in both of these processes. Relax for a while and try to see different hues in your mind. The numbers one through seven are the ones that stand out most clearly in my mind when I try to picture them. Make the color of each number correspond to the Chakra it represents. When you have the number clearly seen in your mind, try first intensifying the color, and then bringing it back down to its original level.

Try to relax; it will become easier, and before long, you will discover that you can do it without putting too much concentration into it. Although it is acceptable to feel a bit annoyed when doing this, since visualization is not something that comes easily to everyone, it is important to remember that this is normal.

Take a comfortable seat, try to relax, and concentrate on how your breath sounds. Maintain your focus on taking long, slow, and deep breaths in through the nose, followed by breaths out through the mouth. Listening to the sound of your breathing is a great way to clear your thoughts.

You now need to center yourself and get a grip.

Creating a foundation

Imagine that you have roots growing from your feet all the way down into the earth now that you have succeeded in calming your thoughts. Sense the energy of the ground rising up via your roots and entering your body through your right foot. This energy is coming from the soil.

Permit the energy to go upwards via your right leg, up through your right side, and as far as the top of your head. Then, allow the energy to flow downwards down your left hand side and out through your left foot before returning to the ground. Imagine this energy as a current that moves from one part of your body to another in a never-ending loop.

Maintain this visualization of the energy, and maintain the flow of the cycle going at all times. You are now confined.

Activation of the Chakras

Now, in order to open the chakras, you need to imagine this current of white energy moving in a slightly different direction. Put your attention on your root Chakra and imagine it as a dull red shape in the form of the number one. (When you have gained more experience with this, you will have the ability to switch it from a number to an image of your choosing.)

Observe how the number goes from having a dull red color to having a vivid red color as the energy fills it. (Your previous experience with visualization will be of use to you in this regard, but it may take you a few tries before you are able to concentrate sufficiently to perfect the talent.) Your Chakra point is becoming more accessible as the color of the number increases. After all of the light has been allowed in, it will fully open.

Keep moving upwards until you reach your sacral chakra and continue the flow of energy. Employ the same method of visualization, but this time with the number 2 in a dull orange color. Increase the brightness of the number, and go higher.

Continue to direct the flow of energy through the subsequent Chakras, checking to make sure that the numbers align with the appropriate colors at each one. After you have successfully opened your Crown Chakra, let part of the energy to flow up through the top of your head, then down around you to fill your aura. Do this until the energy no longer flows through you.

Imagine that the outside borders of the aura are gradually becoming more tangible as you continue to do this. Imagine that this is creating a barrier that only pure good energy can pass through, and that this barrier is preventing any negative effects from entering your body. (By doing this, you will be better able to protect yourself from the powerful impacts that come from other people's auras.)

The remaining fifty percent of your energy stream should be directed such that it flows back into the continuous stream and then back out of your right foot. Maintain the cycle, but this time make a little adjustment to its path so that it runs up and across your Chakra points as it makes its way through the cycle.

www.ingramcontent.com/pod-product-compliance
Lightning Source LLC
Chambersburg PA
CBHW052137110526
44591CB00012B/1764